Thinking on Your Feet

by Linda Kita-Bradley

Grass Roots Press

Thinking on Your Feet
© 2018 Grass Roots Press
www.grassrootsbooks.net

Acknowledgements

Grass Roots Press acknowledges the financial support of the Government of Canada for our publishing activities.

Canadä

Produced with the assistance of the Government of Alberta through the Alberta Multimedia Development Fund.

Alberta

Editor: Dr. Pat Campbell
Photography: Susan Rogers
Book design: Lara Minja, Lime Design Inc.

Library and Archives Canada Cataloguing in Publication

Kita-Bradley, Linda, 1958–, author
    Thinking on your feet / Linda Kita-Bradley; Susan Rogers, photographer.

(Soft skills at work)
ISBN 978–1–77153–226–6 (softcover)

    1. Readers for new literates. 2. Readers—Problem solving. 3. Readers—Decision making. I. Rogers, Susan, 1952–, photographer II. Title.

PE1126.N43K58755 2018   428.6'2   C2017–906940–3

Printed in Canada

Part 1

Angel works in a hair salon.

Angel works for Sara.

Angel's first customer walks in.

Angel shaves his head.

He pays at the front.

Oh no!
The machine is not working.

Angel asks Sara, "Can you help me?"

Angel puts dirty towels in the washer.

She starts the washer.

Angel hears the front door open.

A woman walks in.

She has purple hair.

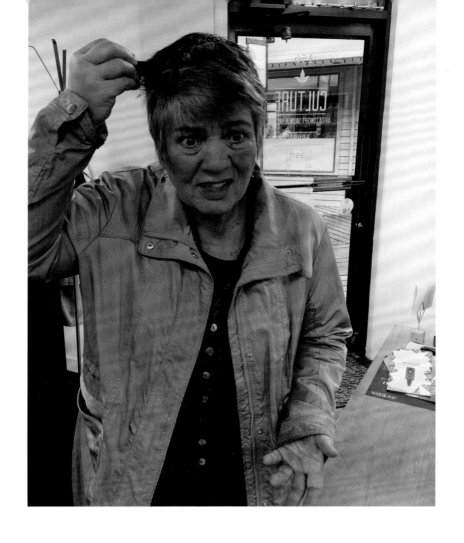

"Help! I used the wrong dye."

"I can't help you.
We are too busy."

The woman leaves the store.
She is upset.

Angel checks the towels.
The washer is not working.

Angel asks, "Can you help me?"

"No. I'm too busy."

Angel needs a cup of coffee.

Oh no!
The pot is empty.

The can of coffee is empty, too.

"What else can go wrong?"

Talking About the Story

1. What does thinking on your feet mean?

2. Imagine you are Angel.

   How do you feel when your boss doesn't help you?

3. Describe a time when you were able to think on your feet.

   Describe a time when it was hard to think on your feet.

Part 2

Read the next story about Angel.
How is it different from the first story?

Angel works in a hair salon.
She works for Sara.

Angel's first customer walks in.

Angel shaves his head.

The customer pays.

Oh no!
The machine is not working.

Angel writes down the card number.

The customer leaves.

Angel checks the machine.
The cord is loose.

Angel puts dirty towels in the washer.

She starts the washer.

Angel hears the front door open.

A woman enters the salon.

She has purple hair.

"Help! I used the wrong dye."

Angel says, "We're busy.
But we can help you tomorrow."

The woman leaves.
She is happy.

Angel checks the towels.
Oh no! The washer is not working.

Angel writes down the serial number.

Angel phones for service.

Sara smiles.
Angel can really think on her feet.

Sara brings Angel coffee.